Sum

of

I'm Still Here
Austin Brown

Conversation Starters

By Paul Adams
Book Habits

Tips for Using Conversation Starters:

EVERY GOOD BOOK CONTAINS A WORLD FAR DEEPER THAN the surface of its pages. Questions herein are designed to bring us beneath the surface of the page and invite us into the world that lives on. These questions can be used to:

- Foster a deeper understanding of the book
- Promote an atmosphere of discussion for groups
- Assist in the study of the book, either individually or corporately
- Explore unseen realms of the book as never seen before

Table of Contents

Introducing *I'm Still Here*

I'm Still Here: Black Dignity in a World Made for Whiteness* by Austin Channing Brown is a book to that will engrave itself in a reader's mind. Austin grew up in predominantly white area and her experiences of being a black female soon taught her a lesson that she has gone on to help others. Brown's words are raw with passion and anger as she writes about her commitment against the white culture and their inherent racism even while trying to go against it. While Brown primarily works through Christian organizations with her talks, faith plays a minor role in *I'm Still Here*. Brown begins her debut through explaining the reasoning of her name, Austin, as her parents wanted her to sound like a white male so she could get more job interviews. Brown writes about how people are always surprised when she walks in and they see a black female instead of the white male they are expecting. This in turn goes into the theme of her debut on how being a black female in a white work place is exhausting to deal with every day. Brown notes that white people are inheritance racist, even if they do not realize it. They are expecting Brown to be white though the white people have not yet realized that their white culture is not the result of rightness, goodness or of the Christian God's blessing. Brown states that white supremacy must be seen for what it is and be named. Only then could the minuscule bit of hope that a community will name whiteness so that they can instead celebrate Blackness will begin to grow. Brown writes about her being part of the twenty percent in a white workforce makes it so she stands out even further, as everyone will know whether she is at a meeting or not. She and her other colored coworkers began to believe that their organization looked more towards having a diverse group while not wanting a diverse culture and thought. Brown defines white fragility and writes about how it is dangerous to others as it ignores the person within people of color and instead makes it so a white person's feelings are more important or even the most important thing to worry about. Now

Brown does realize that there are many kind white people in the world, however that is the problem with racists. Brown writes how the internal structure of racism and how it operates will obligate people like Brown to be nice in return to white people being nice instead of speaking the truth to them. Brown states that white people want to desperately belong to the idea that only cruel white people are racist. However Brown writes that saying that a nice person is racist is offensive to them because it challenges their self-identification, making a white person more worried about being called racist rather than realizing their actions are in fact racist. Brown points out that every KKK member was loved by family members and friends;

a monster is always well dressed and loved by the people it associates with. Brown makes sure readers understand that she is not a priest for a white person to try to absolve their sins. She states that white people really just want a Black person to forgive them, but that white guilt is deadly to a Black person while a white person tries to find their own relief from their actions. Brown then goes on to write about how a Black person can survive racism in an organization that totes they are antiracist. She begins that one should ask specifically why they are being interviewed and looked at to be hired. If the organization's answers do not work with one's reasons for being at that organization, then one should look elsewhere. Once hired, one should make sure that they define their terms of justice, anti-racism and diversity, for oftentimes the organization's version is different. Brown counsels that one should immediately find your people within the organization so that you can band together against racism within the organization. Lastly, Brown states that it doesn't really matter because Blackness will always be offensive to white people. Brown looked towards how white drug dealers and murderers are always seen as people first who just happened to do something wrong, while Black people must be perfect to be seen in the same way. Brown states that she doesn't mean to condemn white people, but her debut is about rejecting the idea and assumption that being white does not automatically make one right, chosen, closer to God, or make one the epitome of a human being.

Discussion Questions

"Get Ready to Enter a New World"

Tip: Begin with questions dealing with broader issues to ensure ample time for quality discussions. Read through all discussion questions before engaging.

question 1

Brown's parents named her a male name to help her in interviews. Do you think that was a good idea? Why or why not?

~~~

question 2

Brown works predominantly with Christian organizations. How do you see this helping her cause?

~~~

~~~

question 3

Brown learned why her parent's named her Austin when she was seven years old. How do you see this knowledge shaping the rest of her life?

~~~

~ ~ ~

question 4

Brown wrote how people were shocked to see a black woman when she walked into job interviews. Do you think her reasoning behind their shock is valid? Why or why not?

~ ~ ~

~~~

question 5

Brown writes that white people are inherently racist even if they do not see it. Do you agree? Why or why not?

~~~

~~~

question 6

Brown writes that white people expect her to be white. Do you think this is true? Why or why not?

~~~

~~~

question 7

Brown states that white supremacy must be named for people to start getting rid of it. How do you think she means that?

~~~

~~~

question 8

Brown wrote about how working in a white-dominated work place made her accountability more noticeable in comparison to her white coworkers. Do you think this is true? Why or why not?

~~~

question 9

Brown wrote that her color wasn't as much as an elephant in the room but rather her secret. What do you think she means by that?

~~~

question 10

Brown wrote how she noticed that many organizations and jobs just hired her to make them seem more diverse in workers. How do you think you would feel in Brown's position?

~~~

~~~

question 11

Brown states that white fragility is dangerous. How do you see that being the case?

~~~

~~~

question 12

Brown states that white people desire the pardon from a Black person. Do you agree? Why or why not?

~~~

~~~

question 13

Brown stated that being a kind person forced a Black person to be kind in return. Do you agree with this idea? Why or why not?

~~~

question 14

Brown wrote how a nice white person is offended by being called racist because it goes against their self-identification. What do you think of this statement?

~~~

question 15

Brown wrote how her book wasn't to condemn white people, but to reject the idea of white supremacy. Do you think she did a good job? Why or why not?

~~~

~~~

question 16

One reviewer stated that Brown's book sheds a new light on racial injustice. Do you agree? Why or why not?

~~~

~~~

question 17

One reviewer stated that every white person needs to read Brown's book to receive some perspective. Do you agree? Why or why not?

~~~

~~~

question 18

One reviewer believes that Brown's book is racist in and of itself. What do you think?

~~~

~~~

question 19

Brown wrote her book so that a Black female will not feel alone in her troubles. Do you think Brown did a good job in that inspiration?

~~~

~~~

question 20

One reviewer stated that Brown's *I'm Still Here* is eye-opening to the world around them. Do you agree? Why or why not?

~~~

Introducing the Author

Austin Channing Brown began her journey when she was a bright eyed and curious seven year- old. While at the library trying to apply for a library card to check out a book, the librarian questioned the girl's name, believing that it wasn't really her name and she was just making it up. Austin felt that librarian become suspicious of her and she ran to grab her parents. Austin's parents confirmed that her name was truly Austin and added that they named her a male's name so that she would be able to navigate the business world easier since it made her sound like a white male. At that moment, Austin began to realize how her darker skin colored made her different in the world she grew up in. Austin worked on her education at North Park University where she earned a bachelor's degree in business management. She continued on with a master's degree from Marygrove College in social justice. Her desire for her degrees was to use them to help make social justice more prominent in her world. She began working for nonprofit organizations, universities, parachurch ministries and churches to help them advance in reconciliation of the socially unjust due for different skin colors. However as she had interviews for various jobs, she always noticed that the interviewer was surprised to see her walk in, a black female, rather than the white male they were expecting. As Austin travels between different organizations to give talks and speeches about racial justice, she worked on her memoir. Published in May, 2018, her debut book and memoir *I'm Still Here: Black Dignity in a World Made for Whiteness* has kicked America for being too white and has stated her position on her thoughts on white supremacy. Austin Brown has become the new leading voice in her desire for racial justice and is committed to have as many workshops for faith, black womanhood and racial integration as she can. Her workshops are touted to being filled with humor, justice, pop culture and of course her personal way of telling the truth without pulling in her punches. Many have stated that while interviewing Austin, they felt a full range of emotions as she celebrated blackness with them. Brown worked on her writing skills as she wrote a column for *Today's Christian Woman* called "Wild Hope". *I'm Still Here: Black Dignity in a World Made for Whiteness* soon became one of Amazon's bestsellers after it was published. Her debut continued its fame with receiving numerous acclaim's from reviewers such as Booklist, Kirkus, and Publishers Weekly. Brown's book was also featured in many other ways such as on BitchMedia, *The Chicago Tribune*, Religion News Service, Popsugar, and more. Brown hopes that with her book, her workshops, and her talks that she will one day live in a world where there is true racial justice.

She hopes that her son will one day see people of color in true leadership positions with actual authority who can influence those around them. She hopes for true diversity in curriculums where Christian churches sing more gospel songs rather than predominantly songs written by white people.

Bonus Downloads
*Get Free Books with **Any Purchase** of* Conversation Starters!

Every purchase comes with a FREE download!

Add spice to any conversation
Never run out of things to say
Spend time with those you love

Get it Now

or Click Here.

Scan Your Phone

Fireside Questions

"What would you do?"

Tip: These questions can be a fun exercise as it spurs creativity among the readers by allowing alternate scene endings and "if this was you" questions.

~~~

question 21

Austin realized why her name was male when she was seven. How do you think she felt when she learned that.

~~~

~~~

question 22

Austin received a bachelors in business management. How do you see that being a part of her later future?

~~~

~~~

question 23

Austin's book made it to the top twenty bestseller list on Amazon. How do you think she felt when she saw that?

~~~

~~~

question 24

Austin wrote a column for a year for *Today's Christian Woman*. How do you see that helping her later in her life?

~~~

~~~

question 25

Austin hopes that one day Christian churches will add more diversity to their music and teachings. Do you think this will happen? Why or why not?

~~~

~~~

question 26

Austin's life for racial justice began when she learned why she was named Austin. What do you think would have happened if she had a more typical female name?

~~~

~~~

question 27

Austin grew up in a predominantly white neighborhood. What do you think would have been different if she lived somewhere else that had more racial integration?

~~~

~~~

question 28

If you were Austin, how would you have handled the librarian who questioned your name?

~~~

~~~

question 29

Austin wrote her debut on how white people can be exhausting. What do you think would be different if she never mentioned about white supremacy?

~~~

~~~

question 30

Austin's book was published by Penguin Random House. What do you think would have happened if her book was never taken in by a publisher?

~~~

Quiz Questions

"Ready to Announce the Winners?"

Tip: Create a leaderboard and track scores to see who gets the most correct answers. Winners required. Prizes optional.

quiz question 1

True or False: Brown tells the story of how she got her name. It was because her grandmother had the same name.

quiz question 2

True or False: Brown has had interviews when the interviewer showed surprise when she arrived. It was because she was a female.

quiz question 3

The first sentence in Brown's book is about living in a white world. It begins with how white people are _____.

quiz question 4

Brown states that in order for change there must be a realization. White supremacy must be _____.

~~~

quiz question 5

True or False: Brown says it doesn't matter if you are kind. White people are inherently racist.

~~~

quiz question 6

True or False: Brown stated that white people are looking for forgiveness from a black person. However Brown states that she is not a priest for the white soul.

quiz question 7

Brown states that nice white people don't like being called racist. It is because it hurts their _____.

~~~

quiz question 8

True or False: Brown began her degree not in social justice. Her bachelors was in business management.

~~~

~~~

quiz question 9

True or False: Brown earned a masters in social justice. She received her degree from Ohio State University.

~~~

~~~

quiz question 10

Brown wrote for a year on a column for an online website. Her column was called _____.

~~~

~~~

quiz question 11

True or False: Brown worked in a different type of businesses after college. She primarily worked for nonprofits, churches and universities.

~~~

quiz question 12

Brown stated that she hopes there will be change within Christian churches. One of the things she wants them to change is for them to sing more _____.

Quiz Answers

1. False
2. False
3. Exhausting
4. Named
5. True
6. True
7. Self-identification
8. True
9. False
10. Wild Hope
11. False
12. Gospel music

Ways to Continue Your Reading

EVERY month, our team runs through a wide selection of books to pick the best titles for readers and reading groups, and promotes these titles to our thousands of readers – sometimes with free downloads, sale dates, and additional brochures.

Click here to sign up for these benefits.

If you have not yet read the original work or would like to read it again, you can purchase the original book here.

Bonus Downloads

*Get Free Books with **Any Purchase** of Conversation Starters!*

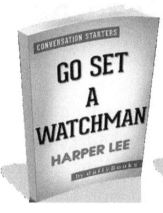

Every purchase comes with a FREE download!

Add spice to any conversation
Never run out of things to say
Spend time with those you love

Get it Now

or Click Here.

Scan Your Phone

On the Next Page...

If you found this book helpful to your discussions and rate it a 4 or 5, please write us a review on the next page.

Any length would be fine but we'd appreciate hearing you more! We'd be very encouraged.

Till next time,

BookHabits

"Loving Books is Actually a Habit"